At an Uncertain Hour:
Primo Levi's War against
Oblivion

Since then, at an uncertain hour,
That agony returns,
And till my ghastly tale is told
This heart within me burns.

S. T. Coleridge
The Rime of the Ancient Mariner

The Menard Press
London
1990

At an Uncertain Hour:
Primo Levi's War against Oblivion

Cover design by Merlin James
Photograph supplied to The Menard Press by Primo Levi in 1976

Distribution in North America by
SPD Inc
1814 San Pablo Avenue
Berkeley, Cal 94702, USA

ISBN 0 9513753 2 6

The Menard Press
8 The Oaks
Woodside Avenue
London N12 8AR
081–446–5571

Typeset by Fakenham Photosetting Ltd
Printed by Short Run Press Ltd

CONTENTS

PREFACE AND ACKNOWLEDGEMENTS

For parts of this book I have revised or recycled my reviews and articles on Primo Levi – in particular an essay on Levi and Celan published in an earlier version in the Jewish Chronicle literary supplement – as well as my contributions to two BBC World Service broadcasts and one BBC Television discussion. Also, two talks: one at a seminar of the Institute of Jewish Affairs/Jewish Quarterly in London, the other at the *Anne Frank in the World Festival* in Nottingham. My thanks to the various editors and organisers. For the brief extracts from Levi's work, I would like to acknowledge his English publishers, in particular Faber and Faber, who now publish the poems originally brought out by Menard. In the interests of continuity I have not glossed or footnoted the details of all references to Levi and others cited in the text, but all conscious sources are listed in the bibliography.

It is a pleasure to acknowledge the help of four friends with whom I have discussed Levi's work at different times: Barbara Garvin, Audrey Jones, Aviva Kipen and, in particular, Ruth Feldman who, in addition to sharing with me over many years some of her special inwardness to Levi's work as his main poetry translator, has supplied me with certain articles from American journals I might otherwise have missed, and has allowed me to read and to quote from her unpublished text: 'Remembering Primo Levi'. Musa 'the Turk' Farhi made some typically sensible comments on a draft of my text. Nick Jacobs, Hyam Maccoby, Ruby Riemer and Norma Rinsler supplied bibliographical information. Edda Thomas loaned me her precious copy of the original 1947 edition of *Se questo è un uomo*. Levi's American publisher very kindly rushed me an uncorrected proof copy of *The Sixth Day*. My thanks to all of them. My thanks too to Lucia Levi for her kindness and friendship.

I have tried to avoid being sentimental about Primo Levi in the main body of the text. Here I briefly permit myself to express the pride I feel in having published Levi's quondam *Collected Poems: Shema* (The Menard Press, London 1976). On politics and other issues I regularly want to consult him. Alas, all I can do now is ask myself: what would Levi have thought about, say, German unification, Israeli policy towards the *Intifada*, the quality of his translators, *my* views on *his* views about Celan. I am troubled by the thought that my text would probably not have been written if he were still alive. But my responsibility, as he would have been the first to stress, is to what I have actually written. I would like to think it is in the spirit of Primo Levi.

I
'STRANGE POWER OF SPEECH'

We all have a private pantheon of writers whose work has changed our lives, whose arrival in our minds and hearts – whether by accident or design or both – affects radically the way we connect our models of inner and outer worlds, forces a readjustment of our private balance between socio-pathological and psycho-pathological explanatory structures, gives us a renewed insight and outsight into what it means to be human. Primo Levi is a member of my pantheon. He wrote at least four masterpieces: *If This is a Man*, *The Truce*, *The Wrench* and *The Drowned and the Saved*, but all his books are essential reading.

I first read Levi in the late nineteen-sixties when for personal and other reasons I became obsessed with the Holocaust[1], a word Levi rightly came to disapprove of, and which I shall try to avoid. I knew at once, as everybody does, that *If This is a Man* is a noble and luminous book. Its author was blessed – as he hoped he would be – with 'strange power of speech', in the Ancient Mariner's own words about himself. Levi identified with the Ancient Mariner, with good reason. *If This is a Man* is the book by which all other writing on this subject is measured – or rather unmeasured – and found wanting; a book whose descriptions of behaviour and attitude would have shaken Dante, Goethe, Diderot; a book whose moral grandeur – *by* understanding *out of* compassion

1

– would have aroused their awe. It is a question of tone, of what Primo Levi did with his anger. Wallenberg too was angry. Sometimes we must contain our anger in order to produce effects. Some people forget this.

That a man who was made to go through what Levi went through can write in the way he does, is itself an act of self-respect and dignity, a sign of strength, a deep reinforcement of the forces which sustain the permanent war against tyranny. It is an act of hope: 'only for the sake of the hopeless ones have we been given hope', wrote Walter Benjamin. It is the work of an anti-fascist militant and partisan. It is, to use a word from Levi's own profession, an antidote to fascism. Chemistry itself is anti-fascist, according to this Jewish chemist, because it can tolerate impurities, life-giving impurities such as carbon, by supplying a literal, metaphorical and conceptual framework for containing impurities, unlike the Nazis who wanted to destroy the allegedly impure people known as Jews. And who is not impure? 'I am the impurity that makes its zinc react, I am the grain of salt or mustard', Levi writes in *The Periodic Table*.

If This is a Man, along with several other books of Levi, is an act of witness, witness for the prosecution of the perpetrators of genocide, and witness for the defence of the victims, especially those who were 'drowned' or 'submerged'. The witnesses come from the ranks of the survivors, every single one an exception Levi insists. This witness managed to turn himself into a participant observer, to stand outside himself and register the suffering passion of a young man caught up in a whirlwind of hate and destruction. The witness's primary act is to tell what he saw, not to stand in judgment. *If This is a Man* is written by a trained scientist, its events were lived by that scientist, and the rest of his life in writing is the fascinating telling of the dialectic between chemist and writer.

So many people who did not know him have said or written that they took Levi's death as a *personal* loss that we should ask ourselves why this is the case. You have to go back as far as Tolstoy to find a precedent. The reason – is it a tautology? – must lie somewhere in the intensely personal matrix of his writing, which yields an amazing integrality of life and work – the life's work and the work's life – and linked to the integrality, integrity. The reader is addressed as a Thou, an unhypocritical semblable whom the author looks straight in the I, as if we were all characters in Levi's title story in *The Mirror Maker*, author and reader reflected in each other's 'metamirs'. The author's voice incarnates his vital interests and beliefs with lucidity and clarity – in fiction, autobiography, poetry, essays. Such a range is rare. Czeslaw Milosz and Octavio Paz spring to mind. Primo Levi, the foremost literary humanist of our time – and how appropriate, even necessary, that he should be a camp survivor *and* a scientist – is in some ways old-fashioned, a classical moralist in the French sense. Yet he is a completely modern writer.

Levi is never afraid to make judgments and yet we trust him because he is so measured and because he is in the business of fine discrimination, above all in the terribly difficult area of moral responsibility, including his own. No survivor was a saint. And Levi does not spare himself. He carries the reader, his brother or sister, with him because he is at once participant and observer and because of the measured tone, the understatement. Only in a late book, *The Drowned and the Saved*, do we become aware that the tone, even if it did reflect his own voice and was not, or was not *only* a literary strategy, had been exacted at a price, but a price on balance worth paying. To reach the heart of reason – understanding – sometimes you will appear in the eyes of fools to be playing down the reason of heart – anger – but you are right to do that. As Goya knew. We shall return to this theme.

Levi's morality is implied by and formed from an old-fashioned compound of reason, tolerance, trust in language, trust in silence, containment of anger, liberalism, cool Sephardi Jewishness, scepticism, good humour, wit and natural philosophy. He told me once that in his opinion one particular writer of the *Churban* was too literary, another was hysterical, not literary enough. This is a clear signal that 'between extremities [he] runs his course', to quote Yeats' "Vacillation", that Levi negotiates carefully between the soul and the heart, to use terms from the same poem of Yeats. In particular he does not trust heavily elaborated literary strategies – despite or even because of his own in *If This is a Man* – and abhors what he sees as rhetorical overkill, which leads him to a rare misreading, namely of Celan, in *Other People's Trades* (which I shall discuss in detail later). It signals that Levi allows and allows for art. Art is what he makes, even lyric poems, on occasion lyric poems *not* about Auschwitz, despite Adorno's dictum (usually quoted without the crucial qualifier 'lyric') – 'I have no wish to soften the saying that to write lyric poetry after Auschwitz is barbaric; it expresses in negative form the impulse which inspires committed literature'. Levi would have been intrigued by Yves Bonnefoy's remark in his essay "Poetry & Truth" that the problem after Auschwitz is not poetry, which knows its own mendacity, but the discourse of ideology, which is prose.

Critics argue the metaphysical question as to whether Levi would have been a writer had he not been incarcerated as a slave, and it is true that he himself said Auschwitz made him a writer. But Levi is not taking sides in the metaphysical dispute. In the camp he actually wrote things down when he could, and then destroyed them. He lived every minute in order, later, to tell. And then, later, he would tell every minute in order to live. One of the most brilliant and enchanting chapters in any of his books is the narrative of an atom of carbon, the last episode in *The Periodic Table*. He gives a strong hint that it was drafted in Auschwitz: 'To carbon, the element of life, my first literary dream was turned, insistently dreamed in an hour and a place where my life was not worth much: yes, I wanted to tell the story of an atom of carbon'.

What is important is what the young man, arrested as a partisan and deported as a Jew, did with his experience in the place where 'ist kein warum' as he was told, 'there is no why', how he survived in the profane and secularised incarnation of inferno, 'Dantesque' in Levi's own word, an inferno such as Dante himself could not have imagined on earth, the same Dante whose work informs many of Levi's books, and the recollection and teaching of whose words to a fellow prisoner forms one of the most affecting and powerful chapters in *If This is a Man*, 'The Canto of Ulysses'. If Levi has to stop reconstructing what he can remember of this Canto (Canto 26) – which has enabled him to understand 'in a flash of intuition, perhaps the reason for our fate, for our being here today' – it is not for the reason that we stop reading Dante when Paulo and Francesca, in Canto 5, in turn stop reading about Lancelot embracing Guinevere and themselves embrace: namely that the greatest poetry has interruption built into it and insists we return to the world (impelled towards a unity ordered by the poetry, a unity including the erotic but not reducible to it however natural and desirable the latter may be, the lineaments of gratified desire embracing reaction to the lover and to the book). Or perhaps it is for that reason.[2] *They have reached the soup queue in the kitchens*. The Ulysses chapter begins immediately after the episode where a kapo wipes his hand on Levi, a human rag. Of the lines which yield his flash of intuition, Levi writes that it was

> as if I was also hearing it for the first time: like the blast of a trumpet, like the voice of God. For a moment I forget who I am and where I am. Pikolo (Jean) begs me to repeat it. How good Pikolo is, he is aware that it is doing me good. Or perhaps he has received the message, he has felt that it is to do with him, that it has to do with all men who toil.

And the lines?

> Consider the seed from which you spring.
> You were not born to live like beasts
> But to seek both virtue and knowledge.[3]

If This is a Man was written in 1946. It is clear from "Carbon" and other signs that the book was not merely 'researched' during the year spent in Auschwitz, or more specifically, in Buna-Monowitz, from February 1944 till January 1945: the very writing of a book was already gestating during that period as well as during the eight months in 1945 which it took Levi to get home, an epic journey described in the sequel to *If This is a Man*, *The Truce*, which itself was not written until many years later – in 1962.

Levi was only 28 when he wrote his first book, one of the key books of the century, matrix and radix of a world lost, a world regained. In it, and forever afterwards, he makes it perfectly clear that he was, absolutely speaking, lucky, and relatively speaking, privileged. He was a chemist. Because he was a chemist he knew some German. That was essential and a matter of luck. But he then made it his business to learn the 'lagerjargon' by exchanging bread for private lessons. Because he was a chemist he was useful, and could be employed part of the time in a laboratory. That too was luck. But he then stole equipment and an alloy which, thanks to hard work and ingenuity and cooperation with his friend Alberto, could be converted into flints and bartered for extra rations which helped to keep him alive. All this is told in more detail in the chapter "Cerium" in *The Periodic Table*. Levi had the support of a civilian worker, Lorenzo, who has a chapter to himself in *Moments of Reprieve*. What emerges from these episodes is that it was *necessary* to be lucky and relatively privileged, but not sufficient. You had to say no. *A survivor was a victim who said no*, an unconscious or implicit theme of many major works of *Churban* literature, like for example Jiří Weil's *Life with a Star*.

Primo Levi was trained to be objective, to observe. He was young but not too young, strong, resilient and he kept his wits. He behaved correctly and sometimes very well. He never betrayed anyone but like all the other survivors he understood that you had to look after yourself or die. No survivor was a hero. Even to be a *mensch* was not always possible. And all the time he knew that he must say no, that he must survive in order to bear witness. This, in a way, was his ideological raft, and we can be grateful in retrospect that he was not a passionate Communist, not a passionate Zionist, not a passionate Orthodox Jew, three of the world views which also, sometimes, served to prevent 'drowning' – assuming always character, temperament and luck. But if he had been, he would have been someone else.

In *The Drowned and the Saved*, the openly angry and often anguished sequel to *If This is a Man* and *The Truce* (and entitled after one of the chapters in the first book, a typical piece of Levi recycling of titles, epigraphs, phrases, episodes – sometimes expanded sometimes contracted) and written forty years after his release, Levi is insistent that all survivors, even the best, were 'an anomalous minority who by prevarications, good luck or abilities did not touch bottom'. I should make clear that he is referring to people like himself, ordinary slaves, not the kapos and other members of the collaborative and official hierarchy.

The camps were organised in such a way that, thanks to enforced delegation of dirty work, the distinction between victims and perpetrators was deliberately obscured, creating the 'grey zone' he writes about in *The Drowned and the Saved*. Man was wolf to man, quotes Levi in *The Truce*. In the "Grey Zone" in *The Drowned and the Saved* Levi discusses the moral problems involved in the behaviour, for example, of the special squads, the Sonderkommandos, who worked on the preparations for and administration of the gas ovens, and virtually all of whose members were themselves gassed after a time. People can see or read the testimony of a rare survivor – whom Levi himself quotes – in *Shoah*, a film Levi wrote me he found 'amazing and cruel'. Sobol in his play *Ghetto* and Jiří Weill in *Life with a Star* also deal with the theme of collaboration or "collaboration". Levi sees the existence of these squads as one of Nazism's most demonic crimes.

Levi, painfully and dreadfully, both for himself and for the reader, thinks himself through and writes himself through the moral problems involved in *any* such survival, but at the same time he *never* obscures the distinction between victims who survived – acting sometimes less than impeccably by omission – and the low and high level perpetrators of genocide through slave labour and gas chambers, yet even the perpetrators are treated as human beings not devils, and some had redeeming features. With the massive credential of *If This is a Man*, Levi in *The Drowned and the Saved* allows that even the worst were not monoliths and might have behaved differently in different circumstances. He charges the Germans with closing their mouths if they knew and their eyes and ears if they didn't. His condemnations are all the more powerful in the light of his discriminations. If he can mitigate he will.

But as one of the 'saved' Levi must speak out *for* the 'drowned' or 'submerged' and *against* those who divided the slaves against each other and ruled over them in a perfected system of totalitarian terror. That such a man should feel shame and guilt at surviving is not the least indictment of the Germans, some of whose attitudes are described in the "Letters from

Germans" (and he means 'Germans' not 'Nazis')
chapter in *The Drowned and the Saved* as well as in
"Vanadium", the famous chapter in *The Periodic
Table* in which Levi describes his correspondence
with the head of the laboratory where he worked for
a few months in Buna, Dr Müller who 'perceived in
my book an overcoming of Judaism, a fulfilment of
the Christian precept to love one's enemies': a percep-
tion Levi passes over in ironic silence. Tullio Regge in
his verbose introduction to *Dialogo* claims Levi
'admitted that he had faked' bits of this story. But he
also claims that on the first occasion they met – in
Regge's house in 1972 – Levi said: 'By the way, during the war I was in a concentration camp': this, in
Levi's home town among educated people, many
years after publication of the second edition of his
first book as a result of which he became famous! I
fear Regge is as unreliable as Levi's main prose translator. In this instance we cannot check the translation
against the Italian text because Regge's introduction is
not in the original edition. "Fake" is milder in American usage than in English and I suspect that we are in
the grey area between fiction and autobiography, and
that Regge is confusing content and subject matter.
And what, I wonder, provoked Levi to make that
conversation stopper about the camp, if indeed he did
say it? Be that as it may, *The Periodic Table* is first and
foremost autobiographical/science fiction – I shall return to this. 'You cannot look into it', says Levi's
wife, 'for literal truth.'

Levi tells his story because he *has* to, to keep himself alive, to keep alive the memory of those who died
in their millions, his own people, and other people.
We shall not forget Hurbinek, the three year old of

10

indeterminate background whom Levi tells of in *The Truce*, who could not speak and who was 'probably born in Auschwitz and had never seen a tree', Hurbinek who 'died in the first days of March 1945, free but not redeemed. Nothing remains of him: he bears witness through these words of mine'. Nazism, Levi writes in *The Drowned and the Saved*, was a 'war against memory' and thus, he is suggesting, his own work is a war on behalf of memory, against oblivion. Tone is of the essence. In the end he seems to have felt that those bearing witness were being ignored. We must hope that he was partly wrong.

Both in his life and his writing Levi saw himself, quite rightly, as the Ancient Mariner and, in *The Wrench*, as Tiresias. He also clearly identifies with the Jewish tradition of telling annually the Passover story as if the events have been experienced personally by those sitting around the table: 'Each of us has been a slave in Egypt', Levi writes in his 1982 poem "Passover" – quoting the Passover Hagada which Jews read each year. We know, for example, from Bassani's *Garden of the Finzi-Continis* that Italian Jews, among the most assimilated in the world, continue to observe at least Passover which, along with Yom Kippur, is the most enduring of Jewish festivals among the non-Orthoprax. Sometimes Levi reminds me of Job, as in the episode of Kuhn and Beppo, one of the few openly angry moments in *If This is a Man*, for truly 'the stones of darkness and the shadow of death' are upon him. And, indeed, *The Search for Roots*, Levi's untranslated anthology of the works that have influenced him, begins with the Book of Job.

In *The Periodic Table* and elsewhere Levi tells how until he had finished writing his book of witness he

11

would button-hole complete strangers in the street. His key poem "The Survivor", which I shall come back to, has as its epigraph, as does the book *The Drowned and the Saved*, a famous quatrain from "The Ancient Mariner".

> Since then, at an uncertain hour,
> That agony returns:
> And till my ghastly tale is told
> This heart within me burns.

Ad ora incerta, "at an uncertain hour", is the title of his collected poems in Italy. On the other hand, the epigraph to *The Periodic Table* and repeated in the text of *The Wrench* and elsewhere is a Yiddish proverb: 'Ibergekumene tsores iz gut tsu dertseylin': troubles overcome are good to tell, the opposite as he points out in *The Drowned and the Saved* of Francesca's remark in *The Inferno* – in the Lancelot passage in Canto 5 – that there is 'no greater sorrow/than to recall happy times/in misery'. Good or bad, angry or calm, the tale had to be told, the *passion* was to tell.

In the actual telling the fires are banked. It would be a defeat to go over the top. And it would be a mistake. Levi trusts in language, in culture, in the values of the old Europe which the Nazis tried to destroy. This restraint is one of the sources of the power of *If This is a Man*. The tone of voice may not have involved a conscious strategy and the writing was certainly a catharsis, even a therapy, but he is a writer not an analysand and writers choose, or are chosen, to present themselves in a certain way to known or unknown readers. In an essay in *Prooftexts* Levi tells us he just wrote because he was fulfilling an obligation and had no 'preconceptions of style', and

Camon reports him as saying he remembers 'writing it without ever faltering' in a few months. But in his interview with P. Roth he is explicit about his style: namely a factory report. And the writing of *If This is a Man* in its very rhythm as well as tone suggests that such a report was indeed his model. Similarly Levi is quite explicit that he chose to conceptualise the camp as a gigantic experiment. At least this is my reading of the sentence towards the beginning of chapter nine "The Drowned and the Saved" (one more example of a phrase later recycled) which is translated as follows: 'We would also like to consider that the Lager was pre-eminently a gigantic biological and social experiment'. F. Eberstadt (see bibliography) wants to read this as a glossing over, on Levi's part, of the genocidal intentions of the Nazis. In the context of the chapter and Levi's style in general it is clear that he is adopting an as-if stance, *a rhetoric to think atrocity*. Eberstadt is way off beam. This way of reporting seems to me to form part of a complex, appropriate and adequate model, a brilliantly organised structure, to enable the saying of the unsayable, the bearing witness of the unbearable. The tone of *The Drowned and the Saved* is another story, the reflection of the price paid in life for the earlier necessary restraint and control.

The rhythm and tone of *The Truce*, written fifteen years after *If This is a Man*, are inevitably different, the author no longer a traumatised convalescent. This book looks forward to *Moments of Reprieve* and *The Wrench* in that its telling of people and events and work are not always shadowed by death. It has its own unity, being for the most part an unexpectedly cheerful record of Levi's eight months' wandering homeward across Europe or, better put, returning to

life after slavery. It describes his purgatory after inferno, his wilderness after Egypt. This most moving
and powerful of travel books tells with wry humour
and keen insight of the turmoil in Eastern Europe
during and after the defeat of the Nazis. The Russians
may not be Italians but they are certainly not Germans. Levi's two books together provide a decisive
counterpoint occasionally explicit, to the historiogra-
phy which would equate Nazism and Communism, a
theme he returns to in an essay in *The Mirror Maker*,
in his conversations with Camon and elsewhere.

The Nazis violated Levi's deepest beliefs and personal morality. Because rebellion is impossible, you
put aside your anger, you store up the outrage, everything must be remembered. A book edited by Myron
Winick, *Hunger Disease*, contains the meticulously recorded accounts, by doctors starving alongside their
patients in the Warsaw Ghetto, of the suffering of the
patients and the doctors themselves, a completely
legitimate medical experiment and their only way to
resist, to defy barbarism. Smuggled out of the ghetto,
their findings are a real contribution to medical literature. These circumstances certainly can never be repeated. Levi too smuggled his findings – hidden in his
memories – out of the camp. But in his retrospective
telling there is a necessary disjunction between what
is described and the way it is described, a disjunction
which opens our minds and educates our hearts.
Some of the implications of this are raised in my discussion of Levi and Celan later. The intellectual and
spiritual ability to stand outside himself and analyse
was an essential mode of survival for Levi. There is
no other way of reading the first book. The way to
survive, in effect, was to write a book in his head.

14

When he comes to write it on paper it is not, therefore, surprising that, like the Ghetto doctors, he goes gentle, is calm and understates: for this is the most effective form of witness. The events themselves scream. If I scream, he seems to be telling us, I shall be violating the very structure and content of the values the Nazis shat on – an image Levi would not disapprove of, given their attitude to bodily functions as described in *If This is a Man*.

Intellectuality and high culture have never been guarantees of humaneness as we know from accounts of certain Nazis, nor an automatic defence against the stones of darkness as we know from accounts of certain victims. Conversely inner strength and an iron will to live were found – it hardly needs saying – among, for example, the stevedores of Salonika whose toughness and solidarity, transformed, will be a theme of Levi's novel, *The Wrench*. Levi himself derived strength and consolation from Dante, the Jewish bible and other canonical texts in world literature. By incarnating the raging storm in an unraging literary form Levi is asking the reader to participate in the work of reconstruction of human values, to help build a wall that will not again fall down. He is quite explicit, for example, about the risk of nuclear omnicide in *The Drowned and the Saved*, *The Mirror Maker*, *The Sixth Day* and elsewhere. *If Not Now, When?* ends with the birth of a child the day the bomb was dropped on Hiroshima.

If Not Now, When?, a book by which Levi set great store, is a 'real' novel, with invented characters, based on real events researched for a year in a library, the happiest year of his life according to Levi. It is possibly significant that – judged by the standards of his

15

masterpieces – this is Levi's least successful book, in some ways a willed book. Levi imagines best out of his own experience. His best characters as such are found in quasi- or non-fiction books such as *The Wrench*; his best fictions are the technologies *in extremis* of *The Sixth Day* as well as some of his personae poems. *If Not Now, When?* sprang out of two obsessions: an obsession with the whole question of resisting with arms, which he couldn't, and an obsession with the (traditionally non-violent) Ashkenazi Jews of Eastern Europe, which he wasn't, and who, as he recounts in *The Truce*, could not believe he was Jewish since he did not speak Yiddish. Some of them finally found themselves in a position to resist the occupier because firstly they were not in a camp and secondly they – sometimes – had the wherewithal, the sine qua non: military equipment.

This fascination with 'the civilisation distilled from . . . the moonstruck world of Ashkenazi Judaism' – moonstruck because he considers that its most refined fruits, 'surreal and subtle', are the 'endless supply of Jewish self-mockery, the proper counterweight to Jewish ritual' – continues in *Moments of Reprieve* and in an important essay in *Other People's Trades*, "The Best Goods". Resistance and self-defence, yes. Aggression and violence, no. Levi rightly condemned the Israeli invasion of Lebanon and would have, again rightly, condemned the handling of the *Intifada*. *If Not Now, When?* is an appropriation of a fraternal tradition, an act of solidarity. I shall discuss the title later. The book has extraordinary moments and it is a rattling good yarn. But the machinery does indeed rattle on occasion.

Like his fellow Sephardi, Elias Canetti, Levi's best

16

writing and most achieved art has been in autobiography rather than fiction – even the hero of the novel *The Wrench*, Faussone, is Levi's alter ego, while the narrator "is" Levi himself. Levi has no pressing need to invent characters. They were ready made, in Auschwitz and in chemistry, Auschwitz being his postgraduate research project. We cannot now go into the fascinating links between autobiography and fiction, between history and myth. As children when we were telling stories we were fibbing weren't we? In romance languages history and story are the same word, virtually so in English too.

Levi's ego does not obtrude in his books, but even the least aware reader must be able to realise what an iron will, what a strong sense of personal worth and validity enabled him to survive, what strength of character kept him going not only in the camp before, during and after his laboratory respite, but also in the years that followed, with that burden of remembrance lying heavy on his heart and mind. Burden it was, as *The Drowned and the Saved* makes clear, as well as the crucial poem "The Survivor", even though Levi rightly describes himself as a 'guiltless victim':

Since then, at an uncertain hour,
That agony returns:
And till my ghastly tale is told
This heart within me burns.
Once more he sees his companions' faces
Livid in the first faint light,
Gray with cement dust,
Nebulous in the mist,
Tinged with death in their uneasy sleep.
At night, under the heavy burden
Of their dreams, their jaws move,

17

Chewing a non-existent turnip.
'Stand back, leave me alone, submerged people,
Go away. I haven't dispossessed anyone,
Haven't usurped anyone's bread.
No one died in my place. No one.
Go back into your mist.
It's not my fault if I live and breathe,
Eat, drink, sleep, and put on clothes.'

(February 4, 1984)

II

'WORK SETS YOU FREE'

It would appear that Primo Levi committed suicide. In the light and shadow of all that I have said so far it is difficult to know what weight to assign to this difficult and painful matter. Much rubbish has been written. I shall try to stay close to the record and to the books, and try always to keep in mind that his life and the actual manner of its living outweigh twelve-[4] millionfold his death and the possible manner of its dying. I used to think it remarkable that Primo Levi, forty years on, wrote a sequel — *The Drowned and the Saved* — which is more angry and anguished than the original masterpiece. I will try to explain why I no longer think this is remarkable. But much of what I am about to write would be the same if Levi had unquestionably died of natural causes or indeed if he were still alive.

As I have already said, Levi describes in *The Truce* how he returned home slowly, how he returned to life slowly. He returned to Italy, to Turin, to the very house he was born in and where he would write his books during the rest of his life, his desk standing where his cradle once stood. Of how many writers is this true, even without an involuntary removal to slavery? Insistent that many people were worse off than him and that, really, he was quite a lucky man, Levi never forgot that some survivors had no homes, families, indeed homelands to return to, for example Eli Wiesel, and that this made their obsessional approach wholly understandable. All the same, life changed radically for Primo Levi in early 1946. He tells us in *The Periodic Table*:

> ... the next day destiny reserved for me a different and unique gift: the encounter with a woman, young and made of flesh and blood, warm against my side through our overcoats.... In a few hours we knew that we belonged to each other, not for one meeting but for life, as in fact has been the case. In a few hours I felt reborn and replete with new powers, washed clean and cured of a long sickness, finally ready to enter life with joy and vigour; equally cured was suddenly the world around me, and exorcized the name and face of the woman who had gone down into the lower depths with me and had not returned. My very writing became a different adventure ... the work of a chemist who weighs and divides, measures and judges on the basis of assured proofs, and strives to answer questions.... It was exalting to search and find, or create, the right word, that is commensurate, concise and strong; to dredge up events from my memory and describe them with the greatest rigour and the least clutter. Paradoxically, my baggage of atrocious memories became a wealth, a seed; it seemed to me that, by writing, I was growing like a plant.

The woman whose name and face were exorcized is clearly the one described in chapter one of *If This is a Man*, just before the transport arrives in Auschwitz:

> Next to me, crushed against me for the whole journey, there had been a woman. We had known each other for many years, and the misfortune had struck us together, but we knew little of each other. Now, in the hour of decision, we said to each other things which are never said among the living. We said farewell and it was short; everybody said farewell to life through his neighbour. We had no more fear.

Thanks to Levi's habit of precise dating of poems we can be certain he met his wife on or just before February 11, 1946 which is both the date and title of this love poem:

I kept searching for you in the stars
When I questioned them as a child.
I asked the mountains for you,
But they gave me solitude and brief peace
Only a few times.
Because you weren't there, in the long evenings
I considered the rash blasphemy
That the world was God's error,
Myself an error in the world.
And when I was face to face with death –
No, I shouted from every fibre.
I hadn't finished yet;
There was still too much to do.
Because you were there before me,
With me beside you, just like today,
A man a woman under the sun.
I came back because you were there.

Only a month earlier, in a poem dated January 9, 1946 but entitled February 25, 1944, Levi wrote a poem which the later poem consciously or unconsciously will echo in the reference to the sun. This poem, whose title is the date Levi and the woman arrived at Auschwitz, also contains unforced references to Dante and Eliot, as his own note in his *Collected Poems* makes clear. It is an extraordinarily poignant, powerful and simple poem: heart-rending and luminous. It announces a hope that will be triumphantly realised in the writing of *If This is a Man*, a realisation perhaps made possible by his meeting the woman whose presence enables him to exorcize the earlier woman of this short poem. The later poem has

21

the foretold woman under an actual sun. The earlier poem has the actual woman under an imagined sun:

> I would like to believe in something,
> Something beyond the death that undid you.
> I would like to describe the intensity
> With which, already overwhelmed,
> We longed in those days to be able
> To walk together once again
> Free beneath the sun.

Levi arrived back in Turin in October 1945. He wrote fourteen poems in the three-month period from December 28, 1945 till March 23, 1946, about a fifth of his entire output. Later he was to say charmingly that this was the first of his two 'attacks' of poetry. 'To put something in its proper place is a mental adventure common to the poet and the scientist', he says in *Dialogo*. In 1983–4 he had the second attack, which he said happened because 'if you succeed in writing a good poem, then you are encouraged to write another one: it is, in chemical terms, an autocatalytic phenomenon – increasing on itself'. This of course is a description not an explanation of what happened!

On January 10 and January 11, 1946, just after the poem about the dead woman, he wrote two of his most intense and powerful poems, the first one clearly reflecting the Ancient Mariner phase before meeting his future wife and getting down to *If This is a Man*. It is a kind of parody of the most important prayer – the "Shema" – in the Jewish liturgy, and ends with a terrible curse (in a later poem he will curse Eichmann. Let no one say Levi was incapable of being unforgiving). The poem, also called "Shema"

22

is, by the way and typically, the epigraph to a book: *If This is a Man*.

> You who live secure
> In your warm houses,
> Who return at evening to find
> Hot food and friendly faces:
>
>> Consider whether this is a man,
>> Who labours in the mud
>> Who knows no peace
>> Who fights for a crust of bread
>> Who dies at a yes or a no.
>> Consider whether this is a woman,
>> Without hair or name
>> With no more strength to remember
>> Eyes empty and womb cold
>> As a frog in winter.
>
> Consider that this has been:
> I commend these words to you.
> Engrave them on your hearts
> When you are in your house, when you walk on
>> your way,
> When you go to bed, when you rise.
> Repeat them to your children.
> Or may your house crumble,
> Disease render you powerless,
>> Your offspring avert their faces from you.

The poem of January 11 tells in condensed form the nightmare – which regularly visited Levi – described at the very end of *The Truce*. The poem itself is called "Reveille" and serves as the epigraph to that book. The Polish word of course means 'get up'.

> In the brutal nights we used to dream
> Dense violent dreams,
> Dreamed with soul and body:
> To return; to eat; to tell the story.
> Until the dawn command

23

Sounded brief, low:
  '*Wstawàc*':
And the heart cracked in the breast.

Now we have found our homes again,
Our bellies are full,
We're through telling the story.
It's time. Soon we'll hear again
The strange command:
  '*Wstawàc*'.

If This is a Man was brought out by a small publisher in a small edition in 1947. It had been rejected by Natalia Ginzberg at Einaudi, says Camon. Levi tells us that it was then forgotten. This is hardly surprising. The world was not yet ready for such an act of witness – which may be the simple explanation for Ginzberg's behaviour. There was a timelag, and then this unique pioneer book was re-published in 1958. Levi added a new chapter and various other things but neither changed nor removed anything already in it. The second edition heralded the second wave of pioneering testimonies: Elie Wiesel's *Night* (1958), André Schwartz-Bart's *The Last of the Just* (1959) and Piotr Rawicz's *Blood from the Sky* (1961)[5], all three written in French, the second and third being novels. But Levi's masterpiece was the first in what has become an enormous literature. The second edition began to sell in its tens of thousands, there were school editions, radio adaptations, translations, and it now counts as a best seller.

Levi does not seem to have written much, if anything, in the fifties: certainly between the original publication of *If This is a Man* in 1947 and the publication of *The Truce* in 1963, the only book to appear was the second edition of the former. What Levi was

24

doing in the fifties was building a life with his loved and loving wife, raising a family, and working at a proper job as an industrial chemist in whose specialised techniques – concerning paint varnish – he would later become a world authority. In 1962 he wrote *The Truce* and was beginning to write his science fiction stories. When pushed in an interview to say what his Paradise (or promised land) might be – perhaps the professional and personal world of *The Periodic Table* – he said: "I don't think *The Periodic Table* describes a paradise unless you call normal life a paradise, which could be the case. If you are happy with daily life, living the life of a *mensch* freely, then yes you can describe it as my Paradiso".

The Truce is, as I have said, in many ways a happy book. Certainly it is an exuberant one, a book of hope and longing, of convalescence and adventure. I am convinced that Levi's long and unsought eight-month journey home was a kind of blessing. He grew back into normal life (normal relative to Auschwitz: occupied eastern Europe was no picnic, even for those outside the camps, as Levi well knew), and sharpened his wits and perceptions to accommodate his exceptionally broad yet focused and unsentimental sympathies for humankind. During those eight months *If This is a Man* was continuing to gestate. Home again, Levi was ready for love and ready for work. Had he gone straight home he might one day have written a book but not, perhaps, a masterpiece of world literature completed within two years of his time in Auschwitz.

In the early sixties, as I have said, Levi began writing his science fiction stories, virtual realities, unsolemn moralities which discuss and predict destructive uses of technology and echo his ongoing concern – after the hitherto worst monster of all – to prevent more and worse monsters begotten by or in the sleep of reason, or excess of reason. Collected in two volumes in Italy and published as *The Sixth Day* in English nearly quarter of a century later, Levi explores the fictional possibilities inherent in what are, fortunately, only metaphysical conceits, disturbing projections of present trends: these include *mnemogogues*, pharmacological 'arousers of memories' (one in the eye, or rather up the nose, for Proust); 'a hormone that inhibits the existential void'; a pill, *versamine*, which can reverse nature, turn dog into counterdog, convert pain into pleasure: 'if pain is life's guardian, pleasure is its purpose and reward' – the character Dessauer could be speaking for Levi himself.

There is a powerfully imagined and beautifully re-told version – *midrash* if you like – of the Golem fable; and several stories about the *mimer*, a duplicator which is 'revolutionary . . . it does not imitate, it does not simulate, but rather it reproduces the model, re-creates it identically, so to speak from nothing . . .'. In the hands of the narrator's friend Gilberto it is extremely dangerous, for Gilberto is 'a noxious Prometheus . . . a child of the century. . . . I've always thought that, if the occasion arose, he would have been able to build an atom bomb and drop it on Milan "to see the effect it would have"'. Gilberto creates a second wife, and the narrator resolves to have nothing to do with 'the melancholy mess'. Gilberto, however, visits him two months later and says it's all been sorted out. About time, says the narrator. 'No, look, you didn't understand me. I'm not talking about myself; I'm talking about Gilberto the first'.

Then, in another story, the American company which patented the *mimer*, brings out a new product, a beauty meter or *kalometer* but the narrator's wife, a plainspoken everywoman, scandalised, says it should be called a *homeometer*, because it measures conformity. Elsewhere the sales rep of the company likens himself proudly to Prometheus. Undoubtedly the myth was crucial to Levi. It is deeply ironic that the etymology of the name Prometheus is – as all science fiction writers from Mary Shelley to Levi must know – "forethinker".

Other projections include: the *psychophant* which measures your inner image, and the *torec* which transmits total experiences not through the sensory organs but directly on the nervous system. Neither hallucination nor dream, it is 'indistinguishable from reality'. There are more than nine hundred titles, categorised under "Art and Nature", "War", "Wealth", etc. Levi explains how the tapes are prepared in the first place and has much fun describing the experiences of people playing them, including one man who puts the tape in backwards. This particular story looks forward to stories like "Time Checkmated" in *The Mirror Maker*.

Levi's imagination and wit are at their most inventive in these stories and in *The Mirror Maker*. As we know, he had already drafted "Carbon" (the last chapter of *The Periodic Table*) in Auschwitz, and several of these stories were written while Levi was drafting *The Truce* in 1962. This is a writer indeed, a fiction writer of the first rank, but a maker of miniatures like his friend Calvino and Borges, not a full-scale novelist. *The Wrench*, a quasi-novel, is a masterpiece but *If Not Now, When?*, Levi's only attempt at a proper novel, is surely his least successful book.

During the sixties and seventies he was writing regularly for *La Stampa*, which published stories and essays some of which have appeared in French in *Lilith* and in English in *Other People's Trades* and *The Mirror Maker*. In the early seventies, he must have started writing *The Periodic Table*, and perhaps *The Wrench*.

Real work, significant work, was of great importance to Levi, both in theory and in practice, and both theoretical and practical work – as we know from *The Wrench* – where work is the active ingredient – and *The Periodic Table* where it is never absent. These are two of the best books ever written on the subject. Through work he retrospectively and singlehandedly demolishes the gates of Auschwitz, though his spirit had been free even while his body was incarcerated, or he would have died: those gates, with their diabolically mendacious motto 'arbeit macht frei': work sets you free. As well as teaching us about the complex relationship between theory and practice – often in a very funny way – he sometimes seems to abolish the difference between art and science, between chemistry and alchemy, between art and work. These are two exhilarating books, mind blowing and mind sweeping. As Levi says, Dante was an astronomer, Galileo a great writer. There is no problem here about two cultures.

I have already mentioned the chapters in *The Periodic Table* on Vanadium and Carbon, the savage irony of the former, the moving and harmonious implications of the latter: to think that a meditation on photosynthesis could help keep you alive and sane, but it did. There is a kind of magical or, better, alchemical realism about Levi's use, in these autobiographical fictions, of universal metaphors derived from the seriously objective structure of the chemical elements – Levi returns to this subject in some essays in *Other People's Trades* and in the least substantial of all his books, *Dialogo*, to which he contributes only 20%. I wrote earlier about the chapter "Cerium" in *The Periodic Table* with its gloss on events in *If This is a Man*. "Nickel" describes the play of work with great love and fascination:

> For that rock without peace I felt a fragile and precarious affection: with it I had contracted a double bond, first in the exploits with Sandro, then here, trying as a chemist to wrest away its treasure. From this rocky love and these asbestos-filled solitudes, on some other of those long nights were born two stories of islands and freedom, the first I felt inclined to write after the torments of composition in high school: one story fantasized about a remote precursor of mine, a hunter of lead instead of nickel; the other, ambiguous, and mercurial, I had taken from a reference to the island of Tristan da Cunha that I happened to see during that period.

These two stories – "Lead" and "Mercury" – are real fables, and remind us of the territory of Calvino and other fabulists. Fable rather than realistic or documentary writing is his forte when it comes to fiction, and this is confirmed by some of the non-*Churban* subjects he writes about in his essays right through to the eighties, for example on bacteria and on gossip in *The Mirror Maker*. The metaphysical possibilities, the sheer entertainment, inherent in extrapolations from science, in pseudo-scientific experimentation, in pushing scientific and technological models or physical structures beyond their natural limits: this is his territory.

There are really only two characters in *The Wrench*, the narrator, in effect Levi himself, and a globetrotting rigger – nicely described by Philip Roth as a blue-collar Scheherezade – Libertino Faussone. Faussone, a familiar compound of types Levi has met, exists only to tell his tale. Indeed the author/narrator and Faussone are two aspects of a single impulse, the impulse to tell, and what is being told is work, the work of telling and the telling of work. As the narrator says – many reviewers, following the blurb, wrongly attributed it to Faussone – 'loving your work represents the best, most concrete approximation of happiness on earth'.

As Faussone tells the life of his work, the work of his life, often in great technical detail but borne along by the exuberance and narrative skill of a personality very different from the narrator's himself, we understand that he and Levi are on a deep level interchangeable, with the art of story-telling and the science of practical engineering requiring similar skills and giving similar pleasures to their creators. Levi's *alter ego* enables the author to convey with great feeling and eloquence the poetry and dignity of real work, he is 'a rigger chemist, one of those who make syntheses, who build structures to order, in other words'. The same part of Levi which admired the Jewish stevedores from Salonika in Auschwitz would have quite liked to be an outdoor artisan.

Arbeit macht frei. Work sets you free. Nazism perfected the bureaucratisation and industrialisation of death. Inspired in part by techniques pioneered in World War One and the morality underpinning it, which brought about millions of deaths, including in particular the Armenians, the *Churban* could only have happened in the twentieth century. The social organisation of the camps was the result of a deal between German heavy industry which needed labour and the SS who wanted immediate death for the slaves. They settled on a work load, diet and conditions that meant a lifespan of three months on average. A regime of terror. The slave labour could be deployed in an 'inefficient' way, with built-in human obsolescence, because there was an endless supply of slaves. The real work of the camps was death, genocide . . . a word coined in 1944 by the Jewish jurist Lemkin to describe Hitler's policy towards the Jews. The Jew was not used primarily for labour: in the factories of death (s)he *was* the primary material of labour. It required the 'vampire metaphysics' which underpinned the total, diabolical, gratuitous 'ontological wickedness' of the Nazis to think up the use of human skin for lampshades and soap. The two phrases in quotation marks are from V. Jankélévitch's ferocious rubbishing of those who rewrite history (washing their hands . . ./by the light of . . .), liars and self-deceivers who play down or ignore the Nazi achievement in Europe, who make their peace with what is wrong. The official work for the most part turned out to be meaningless, the conditions intolerable, yet it was all wrapped up in a most extraordinarily complex set of regulations, administered with terrible cruelty.

These regulations seem almost to have been a deliberate parody of bureaucratic necessity – Jiří Weil's *Life with a Star* also deals with this theme – a way both of normalising the situation *and* of dehumanising the victims in their own eyes and those of their tormentors and torturers so that, as Levi will argue in *The*

Drowned and the Saved, consciences will rest more easy and to murder of a human being will feel like stamping out a cockroach. In the same book Levi will quote his friend Jean Améry as saying that anybody who has been tortured remains tortured. Levi returned home. There will be hope and peace and joy. But there will also be torment (unending or intermittent?) even though Levi himself, unlike many others, had not been brutalised or physically tortured.

He gratefully retired from his job in 1975 which he had begun to feel was deeply incompatible with and unconducive to writing, but which he had believed in and which he had taken very seriously.[6]

During the decade and more between his retirement and his death Levi would write *If Not Now When?*, *The Drowned and the Saved*, *Moments of Reprieve*, as well as some more of the stories or essays found in *Other People's Trades*, *Lilith* and *The Mirror Maker*. He also wrote poetry. In 1981 he published his anthology of the texts which influenced him, *The Search for Roots*. The text is preceded by a diagrammatic sphere, with "Job" at the top and "Black Holes" at the bottom. Four rows of names lead to the black holes from Job. Each has a motto, these mottos are linked, though not syntactically. A rough translation, linking them together, would be: 'Man suffers unjustly; despite that he has stature; he finds salvation through laughter, salvation through understanding'. The first phrase is exemplified by Eliot, Celan, Babel and R. Stern; the second by Marco Polo, Rosny, Conrad, Vercel and Saint-Exupéry; the third by Rabelais, Porta, Belli and Shalom Aleichem; the fourth by Lucretius, Darwin, Sir L. Bragg, A. Clarke. We shall return to Celan later.

32

Levi was a man of the world, a political animal, if not a party political animal. On another spectrum he is "prophetic" rather than "utopian". I put to him an old chestnut of my own: would democratic socialism be the secular version of Jewish messianism? He replied: 'I do not see any contradiction. I am basically a socialist, though not a member of the PSI. I believe in mutuality, community and a slow progress towards the messianic age'. The key word there is 'slow'. He had already written *The Drowned and the Saved* when he said that. One of the most important points made in that book is that people do not speak out even when it is safe to do so, the Germans being only the most obvious and extreme example. To speak out is indeed our best memorial to him.

I have already said that he was deeply preoccupied with the atomic threat -- social organisation after a nuclear war inevitably manifesting itself as a radioactive concentration camp – and Levi's educated readiness to learn from the singularity of the *Churban* and project into the future its main social and industrial features is one of his crucial achievements as a writer. About Chernobyl he wrote to me in May 1986 that the explosion 'has been not only a tragedy, but a terrifying message too. Everywhere in Europe the man in the street has understood it. Let us hope the masters of the world understand it too'. He quite rightly loathed the policies of Sharon and Begin and got into hot water with the Jewish establishment in Italy over his speaking out against Israel's invasion of Lebanon, though unlike his friend Natalia Ginzberg he did not, in effect, disown Israel and Judaism. *The Mirror Maker* contains an essay on the nuclear issue dated 1981 in which he identifies our denial of the nuclear threat with the denial by the Jews of their predicament which Appelfeld writes about in *Badenheim 1939*, and claims that Appelfeld does this sub-textually – which I am not so sure. But in the final essay of *The Mirror Maker* he refuses to follow the advice on a lapel button – which he read in Martin Ryle's Menard pamphlet – to 'stop science now'.

And so I return to my earlier surprise that *The Drowned and the Saved* is an angrier and less calm book than *If This is a Man*; Levi was a man possessed but he had managed to think other thoughts and do other things than Auschwitz. Nearly forty years on but before the period of hope ushered in by Gorbachev's initiation of genuine but high-risk reforms, it was perfectly clear to any thinking person of goodwill that our planet was tormented and divided, that the hopes of the early post-war years had died in the maelstrom of: ecological irresponsibility on the grandest scale, wars, terrorism, genocide, mass disappearances, unreconstructed political economies, and the rewriting of history. Levi's own political anxieties and analyses interlocked with his original season in hell. This accounts for the urgent tone of *The Drowned and the Saved*, as if he felt his act of witness had not been heeded.

The Drowned and the Saved is an extraordinarily powerful and anguished re-examination of his life-long themes, using every literary ounce and every scientific molecule of the trained intelligence of one of the cleverest and most rounded writers of our time, for whom the "two cultures" was not a problem but a generative matrix, because he brought them together organically, dialectically. And there's a lesson for all of us. But even Primo Levi can contradict himself, significantly in one of the most highly charged of all his themes: on the one hand he writes that 'the just among us ... felt remorse, shame and pain for the misdeeds others had committed', on the other hand: 'the worst survived'. With hindsight we pay particular attention when he writes that suicide is premeditated, borne from a feeling of guilt. As for the SS, 'they were average human beings, averagely intelligent, averagely wicked: save for exceptions, they were not monsters, they had our faces, but they were reared badly'. He is not psychologising. We believe a man who distinguishes shades of grey but always stands firm when it is correct to do so. Who has not given careful consideration to Levi's account of the Jewish Sonderkommando cannot call himself or herself educated in morality or ethics.

The Drowned and the Saved, like all Levi's work is aimed directly at our consciences. Heart and brain must act in unison. This collection of related essays is a coherent whole, a writer's book, a non-fiction fiction, for the author – beneath the real life personae or masks of survivor witness, of secular Jewish humanist, of Italian chemist – speaks from the centre of a validated life without projection, thus giving the sense and feel of a *voice*, which paradoxically you rarely find outside actual fiction. In this case the voice is that of a mensch-in-the-street, a thinking person of goodwill, a decent human being.

The *Pirke Avoth, the Ethics of the Fathers*, is one of the most wonderful books in *The Talmud*. This collection of wise sayings contains, among others, the words of Rabbi Hillel, traditionally the teacher of Jesus. Levi found the title of *If Not Now When?* in a famous phrase of Hillel. One of the sayings of the

35

great Pharisee sage, eschewing both macho individualism and rampant collectivism, and finding the right balance between socio- and psycho-pathological models, goes: 'If I am not for myself, who will be for me? If I am only for myself, what am I? And if not now, when?' Also, in *Pirke Avoth* we find: 'In a place of no men, strive to be a man'. That is, a *mensch*. The life and death of a *mensch*.

It is a matter of public record that in the last year of his life Levi was on anti-depressants until his prostate operation, and he and his wife had been deeply preoccupied with the difficult filial responsibility of care for two nonaganarian mothers. He wrote to Ruth Feldman that he got no rest, day or night. There were other worries too. In his last letter to Ruth Feldman, the translator of his poems, a month before his death, he wrote that he was deeply depressed and was living through a period worse than Auschwitz partly because he was no longer young and resilient. He signed off 'de profundis'. A couple of months earlier he wrote to me that because of personal troubles he was neglecting 'almost everything not connected with mere day to day survival'.

And so, if one places the local history of his life in the context of his general political disillusionment, of his sense of failure, of his specific feelings about Auschwitz, with the latter's intimate dimension of trauma and regular nightmares as recorded both in the first words (the epigraph) and the final paragraph of *The Truce*; if we remember that through the bearing of witness and in the cause of education he – again and again over forty years, in public and in private, in writing and lectures and even by visiting Auschwitz with groups, and latterly reliving the past yet again to

36

help a biographer – returned to the commemoration of unknown victims, lost companions and survivor friends (some told for the first time in the lovely little book of paralipomena, things left out, *Moments of Reprieve*); if we recall that even the best such as himself had to transgress Hillel's dictum and had sometimes to be only for themselves and therefore never got over the feeling of guilt (when quizzed about such episodes Levi, understandably, correctly and rightly, would make a tenacious defence of the selectivity, and this may be why even a Rumkowski is written about with understanding in *Moments of Reprieve* and elsewhere); if we remember the forty years of torment and anger finally released in the words of *The Drowned and the Saved*; if we remember all these things we shall not be surprised that things may have got too much for Primo Levi and that the likelihood is he threw himself from the fourth floor down the stairwell. The values which had once sustained the best of Europe, values which he exemplified and whose collapse he chronicled, could not in the end, alas, sustain him.

Some speculations have been impudent or stupid or both. William Styron for example psychologises on the basis of incorrect facts. Some people ask why this chemist, if he did commit suicide, did not use a less messy technique, a chemical one for example: do they not stop to recall that millions of slaves died by a chemical technique? Or, if that counterexample was *not* in Levi's mind, to consider that the *method* is in any case not of prime importance? Other people talk of a will to self-destruction or a sudden uncontrollable impulse: both these "explanations" are either meaningless or tautological or evasive. And for sure the professor in Turin was wrong who claimed that Levi's suicide was a political protest like that of Jan Palach. The New Yorker plumbed the depths in an unsigned article when it suggested that 'the efficacy of all his words had somehow been *cancelled* by his death'. This outrageous suggestion is of course the opposite nonsense to the idea much peddled, namely that Sylvia Plath's suicide *confirmed* the efficacy of all her words in those blazingly powerful final poems. For supposed premeditation to be relevant to an assessment of Levi's or anyone's work, the critic must show that the work itself is coloured by that matter. Levi's *corpus* breathes life: it is "atemwende", breath-turning, to use the word Celan coined and which I shall return to. To have written *If This is a Man* is in itself as life-affirming an act as can be imagined.

I too feel, I hope without justification, that I have intruded upon private matters. In the final analysis, Levi's death and its likely manner by his own hand are not our business: they are a private tragedy for his family and intimates. Let readers be grateful, let readers rejoice that such a man, with his life's companion, found the strength after Auschwitz to live and to work and to play and to bear witness 'by his own hand' for more than forty years before, perhaps, he despaired. The possible manner of his dying neither cancelled nor validated his life's work, his work's life. With hindsight we may find an early comment of Levi's disturbing and suggestive. One of several references to suicide in Levi's work, it comes in the last chapter of *If This is a Man* written, like all his books, in the fourth floor flat where he was born, lived and died: 'to fall ill of diphtheria in those conditions was surely more fatal than jumping off a fourth floor'.

But even this is irrelevant to a life lived more fully and more meaningfully than most. In the words of the old Roman proverb, may the earth rest lightly on his bones. 'The words of his mouth' wrenched from 'the meditations of his heart' – to adapt the psalmist – are his legacy to Europe and to the world. Rabbi Tarphon, quoted in *Pirke Avoth*, says: 'The day is short and the master of the house is urgent. It is not your duty to complete the work but nor are you free to desist from it'. Primo Levi did not desist.

III
'THE SHORELINE OF THE HEART'

Other People's Trades is a fascinating collection of essays in which Levi sets foot on 'the bridges which unite the scientific and literary cultures'. The real bridge is Levi's mind which properly identifies the two cultures as one. We know from *The Wrench* how much he loves bridges. In *Other People's Trades* Levi explores 'the bonds which link the world of nature to that of culture'. He writes on plant life, animal life, shops, exams, quirks, childhood, professional skills, literature, the spirit of place, toys, pavements, chess, chemistry – glossing *The Periodic Table* – and Ashkenazi Judaism, glossing *If Not Now, When?*. "Signs on Stone", a beautiful and witty meditation, including a disquisition on chewing gum, begins with Dante's quote from the Psalms: 'Adhaesit pavimento anima mea'. The book *works*, that is *plays*. Levi educates us by his very style, that of the common reader who is an uncommon writer, redeeming clichés, resurrecting dead images, reordering familiar taxonomies, abolishing or crossing frontiers in a cheerful yet purposeful way. It reads sometimes as if the wonders of Borges have been crossed with the signs of Barthes.

The parallel with Borges is instructive. Borges is an alchemist, Levi a chemist; Borges an astrologer, Levi an astronomer; Borges is a cabbalist, Levi a talmudist; Borges is a fabulist, Levi a factualist. Yet each is

41

'metamirrored' (to adapt Levi's word) by the other. (I don't know if Borges actually read Levi but Levi certainly read Borges: see "Inventing an Animal" in *Other People's Trades*; and even if Levi had never mentioned Borges by name in an essay you could not fail to detect the influence.) They meet, shake hands at the interface of their two poles. Two of the most insatiably curious writers who ever lived, they never cease to be amazed at the vicissitudes of the human condition, the peripeteia of the human destiny, the avatars of the human project. And both, in their different ways, negate the fashionable idea that the author is not a human being, his text not the product of a mortal, ethical person.

When discussing *The Periodic Table* I said earlier that fable or metafiction is Levi's strength when it comes to fiction, rather than the more conventional narrative of *If Not Now, When?*. Some of the stories in *The Sixth Day*, *The Mirror Maker* and *Lilith* are virtually consubstantial with some of the essays found also in *The Mirror Maker* and in *Other People's Trades*, hence too the presence of fables in *The Periodic Table* amidst the quasi-autobiographical essays whose own structuring principle is that ultimate fiction: the table of chemical elements. Levi, as I once predicted in a review, is indeed closer to the fabulists – Borges, Barthelme, Calvino, Perec – than might once have been supposed. His sporadically fabulous gift was implicit in his delight in unusual and peculiar natural and social phenomena.

One of the stories in *The Mirror Maker* which would have delighted Borges is "Time Checkmated" in which thanks to a patented chemical injection subjective time can be speeded up or slowed down, depending on your needs or desires, by placing the client in 'the parachronic mode'. The title story elaborates on the invention of a mirror maker: 'a meta-mir, that is a metaphysical mirror, does not obey the laws of optics but reproduces your image as it is seen by the person who stands before you. . . . He noticed that no two images coincided; in short a real Timoteo did not exist. . . . Every attempt at commercial exploitation failed'. I shall mention here only one of the essays, "On Translating Kafka" where Levi tells us that in his own writing 'I've always striven to pass from the darkness into the light . . . Kafka forges his path in the other direction'. If you substitute Celan for Kafka you have in a nutshell Levi's complex relationship with his great contemporary's work. It is the relationship between Levi and Celan which I propose to explore in the rest of this section.

There is one essay in *Other People's Trades*, perhaps the only occasion in any of his books, where Levi's touch seems to desert him. The tone is uncertain. He is perplexed. Normally, when he does not understand a phenomenon, he is up front about it, and the subsequent discussion enlightens us. Not here, or at least not in the way he imagines.

In "On Obscure Writing" Levi begins with a characteristic call for sanity, reason and respect for the reader. He then tells us that 'the two least decipherable German poets, Trakl and Celan, both died as suicides . . . Their common destiny makes one think about the obscurity of their poetry as a pre-killing, a not-wanting-to-be, a flight from the world of which the intentional death was the crown'. By 'German' Levi is presumably referring to the language they wrote in, though he also describes Celan as a German

43

Jew; but Trakl was Austrian and Celan was born in Romanian Bukovina in 1920, not long after the break up of the Hapsburg empire, a multilingual Jew who chose to write in German.

Levi admits Celan's song 'is tragic and noble' but then goes on to say that his obscurity is 'a reflection of the obscurity of his fate and his generation'. He should be 'pitied rather than imitated'. Then the key sentence: Celan's 'is a dark and truncated language precisely like that of a person who is about to die and is alone, as we all will be at the point of death. But since we the living are not alone, we must not write as if we were alone. As long as we live we have a responsibility: we must answer for what we write, word by word, and make sure every word reaches its target'.

It is dangerously speculative and significantly wrong, it seems to me, to suggest that the alleged 'dark and truncated language' is a sign of Celan's intended suicide otherwise Levi himself should have been using similar language or alternatively would not himself have committed suicide – which is the likeliest though not certain explanation of his death. More importantly, Levi has, I believe, failed to appreciate the nature of what he calls Celan's obscurity. Celan *is* a very difficult poet – unlike Trakl as it happens – but he is not hermetic or obscure, his language far from dark or truncated. He is, I would say a *necessarily* difficult poet.

The felt experience of reading Celan, of making the effort to understand him, of wrestling with his daemon, just as he himself did, brings serious rewards of insight. Celan is that kind of writer. He is that kind of writer – for two reasons, one of which

Levi does not explore because, precisely, he Levi is *not* that kind of writer. Levi trusted language. In a fascinating essay called "Beyond Survival" Levi makes a remarkable statement: 'I must make clear that neither in *If This is a Man* nor in any subsequent books did I ever face problems of language'. He says this in spite of his early acknowledgment in that first book that 'our language lacks words to express this offence, the demolition of a man' and he says this in spite of a third important statement on the matter of language, in the essay "Rhyming on the Counterattack" in *The Mirror Maker*: 'Since poetry is intrinsic violence done to everyday language, it is understandable that every true poet feels the drive to become a violator, that is, an innovator, in his own right: to invent his own poetics, which stands in relation to the reigning poetics as the latter stands to prose'. And yet another, reported by Camon, namely that although the problem of language was of no interest when he wrote *If This is a Man* 'it gradually began to interest me the more I went on writing, until it became uppermost in *The Wrench*', which contradicts the statement in "Beyond Survival". In spite of the contradiction, what is important is that the trust was always there. Levi proceeds, notwithstanding the early and the late and quite different qualifications to his admitted non-problem, to find the words.

Celan too, finds the words, but in a different way, for he *does* face problems of language, and he might have had he written in any language; once again, he is that kind of writer. But he wrote in German. And this is the other reason why Levi gets him wrong. Whether or not language in general was a problem for Levi or was or was not needed or wanted to be a problem, in some respects even German was not: by knowing it as a chemist, by having the wits to acquire – at a price – the ugly camp jargon, he saved his life. I think language in general was a problem for Paul Celan, or needed or wanted to be a problem, but what is absolutely certain is that German was. Whatever the extent or nature of the problem for both of them, the heart of the matter is *trust*.

The problematic of German was itself a major theme of Celan's work. Though he said the language was all he had, he talks of 'the thousand darknesses of death-bringing speech'. He worries away at the language used and contaminated by those who murdered his mother and a third of his people. He wrestles with it, argues with it, uses it to interrogate and also to reconcile Yiddish, the language of the dead; Russian, the language of his emblematic poet Mandelshtam and of his early political idealism; and Hebrew, the language of the country he does not leave Europe for.

The Nazis contaminated everything, including language, that repository of culture, thought and feeling; language, that mode of I/Thou dialogic in which lovers speak; language, the I and I, if not the we, of nation speaking peace unto nation. To decontaminate and to redeem the language Celan used violent shock treatment. Elements and registers which all poets in all languages at all times exploit on occasion – unexpected etymological renewal, shaken metre, broken rhyme, fractured syntax, violent enjambement, neologisms, archaisms – Celan uses regularly and, as the years go by, privileges. He was not a solipsist. But he believed that 'reality is not. It must be searched for and won'. And 'I have tried to write poetry

46

in order to acquire a perspective of reality for myself'. Levi proceeds in the opposite direction.

Celan's early and most famous poem, "Death Fugue", works more traditionally, as the title suggests. Levi actually includes this poem in his anthology *The Search for Roots*, which I described earlier. In a note Levi says that this is one of the few poems of Celan that he understands. He is moved by it to the point of writing: 'I bear it within myself like an implantation'. But even here Levi goes on to criticise Celan for writing only for himself or for a few, in a coded form to which the poet alone has the key, and he speculates – reasonably enough, and poignantly, but not proving the connection with Celan's way of writing – that the accumulating burden of pain and grief led to Celan's suicide in 1970. If Levi himself can speculate about Celan, then our own attempts to understand Levi's apparent suicide are legitimated.

In "Death Fugue" there is the most radical disjunction between the haunting beauty of the language and the extreme situation described, or perhaps I should say mythologised, made into music. Celan came to reject this hypnotic poem and it is ironic that Levi was so strongly in favour of it given his views on literary strategy and rhetoric. Reversing Yeats I would say that the reason for Celan's rejection was that having given birth to a terrible beauty he realised that all must be changed, changed utterly. The disjunction between language or form and subject matter was, he felt, immoral. Henceforth he must take the language apart, and only by doing this is he permitted or enabled to deal with these themes.

Primo Levi, trusting language, especially Italian, salvaged and reasserted truth through language, went *with* its grain. His life's work and work's life was to *say*. Celan, not trusting language or not trusting German, salvaged and reasserted truth *against* language, went *against* its grain. His life's work and work's life was to *unsay*. They are, both of them, breathtaking and breathgiving writers, *breath-turning/atemwende*, to use the word Celan coined.

We are not obliged to choose between them. On some level each of them contains the other and indeed we all, writers and readers, surely move back and forth between those poles during a lifetime. To read these two virtual contemporaries – born within sixteen months of each other – who are surely the greatest and most exemplary writers of the *Churban*, is to reinforce and perhaps explain both Levi's comment in *The Drowned and the Saved*: 'The aims of life are the best defence against death, and not only in the camp' and Celan's line: 'I hear they call life our only refuge'. It is to contradict with dignity and respect Celan's verses: 'No one/bears witness for the/ witness' and to contradict them in the spirit of the poem in which he quotes, in the original Hebrew, Isaiah's 'arise/shine'//'kumi/ori', and in the spirit of another line: 'there are still songs to be sung on the other side of mankind'.

Paul Celan wrote in a speech: 'A poem, being an instance of language, hence essentially dialogue, may be a letter in a bottle thrown out to sea with the . . . hope that it may wash up somewhere, perhaps on the shoreline of the heart'. Levi, more optimistic, wrote, as I said earlier, that we must 'make sure every word reaches its target'. His writing reflects the 'confidence of the tree in the fruit' to borrow a phrase from a poem of Edmond Jabès. There is a real and honourable difference between Primo Levi and Paul Celan. I doubt that one could construct an argument which might somehow bridge that difference – how sentimental of me even to suggest it. And so, having brought them together, I raise my eyes from the pages of their books ('quel giorno più non vi leggemmo avante' as Francesca says to Dante, that day they read no further) and leave them for the time being, shaking hands on the shoreline of the heart.

NOTES

1. In common with some other writers I shall use the term *Churban*, a Hebrew word for "destruction" and one not laden with the wrong religious connotations of "Holocaust" or even "Shoah". "Ch" is pronounced as in "loch" not "church".

2. This brief discussion is my gloss on Yves Bonnefoy's reading of the Canto Five episode in "Lever les yeux de son livre" (see bibliography) and on a conversation with Gabriel Josipovici and Brian Cummings.

3. This is my own translation negotiated with Barbara Garvin as a result of dissatisfaction both with Sinclair's version and the version in *If This is a Man*. Charles Sisson's version reads:

   > Consider then the race from which you have sprung:
   > You were not made to live like animals,
   > But to pursue virtue and natural science.

   Levi must have understood the paradox, indeed the irony, of remembering these particular lines, given that their speaker, Ulysses, is using them with intent to deceive his comrades. In later years, if not at the time, Levi would also have known that this passage is crucial to the long-running dispute among scholars and readers as to whether Dante, like Milton, was or was not of the Devil's party. Part of the fascination of Dante for some modern readers like Josipovici, and perhaps even a condition of the poet's greatness, lies in the tension held between the two possibilities in the text.

4. The figure "twelve million" perhaps needs glossing. Originally I wrote "six million" – which requires no explanation – then, at proof stage, I thought that this was a good opportunity, and in the spirit of Levi himself, to commemorate *all* the civilians who died at the hand of the Nazis

in concentration camps, not only the Jewish ones. (The figure is rounded down and taken from Martin Gilbert's *Jewish History Atlas*, Weidenfeld and Nicolson, 1969.)

5. Wiesel's and Schwartz-Bart's books are deservedly well known. Rawicz's book, perhaps the only major text of *Churban* literature which has not been paperbacked, is a remarkable and neglected novel. I hope one day to write about the man and his work. He shot himself in 1981.

6. I think Levi exaggerates, in his interview with Roth, the incompatibility. A careful reading of various interviews and uncollected articles reveals inconsistencies, contradictions and even a tailoring of his views for a particular audience. He was off duty. Even his book of conversations with F. Camon (who says Levi checked everything) is not as carefully organised or as accurate as the interviewer thinks. For example, the discussion about the rejection of the manuscript of *If This is a Man* is very confused. Like *Dialogo*, *Conversations* should really be included with Levi's occasional, off-duty, writings rather than with his books.

BIBLIOGRAPHY

1. Books by Primo Levi in English translation

Note: the books are listed in order of original Italian publication.

If This is a Man/The Truce, trs. S. Woolf, Abacus Sphere, 1987 (1947/1963).
Note: this edition contains 'The Author's Answers to Readers' Questions'.

The Sixth Day, trs. R. Rosenthal, Michael Joseph, 1990 (1966/71).

The Periodic Table, trs. R. Rosenthal, Abacus Sphere, 1986 (1975).

The Wrench, trs. W. Weaver, Abacus Sphere, 1988 (1978).

Moments of Reprieve, trs. R. Feldman, Abacus Sphere, 1987 (1981).
Note: the original Italian book *Lilith* from which this selection is taken has been translated in its entirety into French, and published by Liana Levi, Paris 1987.

If Not Now, When?, trs. W. Weaver, Abacus Sphere, 1987 (1982).

Collected Poems, trs. R. Feldman/R. Feldman & B. Swann, Faber & Faber, 1988 (1984).

Dialogo (with Tullio Regge), trs. R. Rosenthal, I.B. Tauris, 1989 (1984).

Other Peoples' Trades, trs. R. Rosenthal, Michael Joseph, 1989 (1985).

The Drowned and the Saved, trs. R. Rosenthal, Abacus Sphere, 1988 (1986).

The Mirror Maker, trs. R. Rosenthal, Methuen, 1990 (1986).

Conversations with Primo Levi, trs. T. Shepley, The Marlboro Press, 1989 (1987) and Penguin (forthcoming).

2. Book by Primo Levi Untranslated into English

La ricerca delle radici, Einaudi, Turin 1981.

3. Other Texts by Primo Levi

'The Sunflower' in *The Sunflower* by S. Wiesenthal, Schocken Books, NY, 1976.
Note: this is Levi's contribution to a symposium on a text by Wiesenthal.
'Beyond Survival', *Prooftexts* (Baltimore), Vol 4/1, January 1984, pp. 9–21.
Interview by Germaine Greer, *Literary Review* 89, November 1985.
Letter in *Commentary*, February 1986.
Note: this is Levi's reply to the egregious F. Eberstadt (see below, section 4).
Interview by Philip Roth, *The New York Times*, October 12, 1986.
Note: 1, The same issue contains Alfred Kazin's review of *The Wrench*. For other reviews of Levi see below. 2. Roth's interview was published in a revised form in *London Review of Books*, October 26, 1986.
Interview by Anthony Rudolf, *London Magazine*, Vol 26/7, October 1986.
Interview by Ian Thomson, *Poetry Nation Review* 58, Vol 14/2, 1987.
Letters to Ruth Feldman and Anthony Rudolf.

4. Articles and Reviews about Primo Levi

F. Eberstadt, 'Reading Primo Levi', *Commentary*, NY, October 1985.
D. Denby, review article on several books, *New Republic*, Washington, July 28, 1986.
J. Lowin, 'Primo Levi's Unorthodox Judaism', *Jewish Book Annual* 45, 1987–8.
A. Stille, 'Primo Levi: Reconciling the Man and the Writer', *New York Times Book Review*, July 6, 1987.

R. K. Angress, review article on two books, *Simon Wiesenthal Centre Annual*, Vol. 3, 1987.

A. Rudolf, review of *The Wrench, Jewish Chronicle*, May 15, 1987.

P. Bailey, Radio Three talk on Levi, BBC, July 30, 1987.

C. Ozick, review of *The Drowned and the Saved, New Republic*, March 21, 1988.

C. Angier, review of *The Drowned and the Saved, New Society*, April 8, 1988.

C. James, review of *The Drowned and the Saved, New Yorker*, May 23, 1988.

K. Miller, review of *The Drowned and the Saved, London Review of Books*, August 4, 1988.

A. Rudolf, reading of Lanzmann's *Shoah* (tribute to Levi), Menard Keepsake 8, 1988.

W. Styron, 'Why Primo Levi need not have Died', *New York Times*, December 19, 1988.

W. Wilde-Menozzi, 'A Piece you've Touched is a Piece Moved', *Tel-Aviv Review*, Vol. 2 (annual), Autumn 1989.

J. Senker, 'Primo Levi: Chemistry, Writing and the Holocaust' (unpublished essay for Philosophy Dept., Leeds University), 1989.

A. Rudolf, review of *Other People's- Trades*, Poetry Nation Review, 73, 1990.

5. Paul Celan (& Trakl)

Speech-Grille and Selected Poems, trs. Joachim Neugroschel, Dutton, NY, 1971.

La rose de personne, trs. Martine Broda, Le Nouveau Commerce, Paris, 1979.

Sixty-Five Poems, trs. Brian Lynch & Peter Jankowsky, Raven Arts Press, Dublin, 1985.

Collected Prose, trs. Rosmarie Waldrop, Carcanet, Manchester, 1986.

Poems of Paul Celan, trs. Michael Hamburger, Anvil Press, 1988 and Penguin, 1990.

Translating Tradition: Paul Celan in France, Acts 8 & 9 (special issue ed. B. Hollander), San Francisco, 1988.

Note: this issue of *Acts* contains an essay by John Felstiner. His essays on Celan are crucial to an understanding of this poet and one awaits with impatience his forthcoming book: *Translating Celan, the Strain of Jewishness*. The edition of Celan translated by Michael Hamburger is the latest of several by him. All English readers of Celan are in his debt. They are equally indebted to George Steiner.

Schibboleth pour Paul Celan, Jacques Derrida, Editions Galilée, 1986.

Trakl: Selected Poems, bilingual, ed. C. Middleton, Jonathan Cape, 1968.

6. Some of the Other Texts Cited, Mentioned or Consulted

T. W. Adorno and others, *Aesthetic & Politics*, NLB/Verso, 1977.

A. Applefield, *Badenheim 1939*, J. M. Dent, 1981.

P. Auster, *The Art of Hunger*, The Menard Press, 1982.

G. Bassani, *The Garden of the Finzi-Continis*, Harcourt Brace, 1977.

W. Benjamin, *Gesammelte Schriften*, (1:I, p. 20), 1974.

Y. Bonnefoy, 'Lever les yeux de son livre', *Nouvelle Revue de Psychanalyse* 37, 1988.

——, 'Poetry and Truth', *Poetry World* (Bonnefoy issue, ed. A. Rudolf) 3, 1990.

A. Cohen, *The Tremendum*, Crossroad, 1981.

Dante, *The Divine Comedy* (Inferno), bilingual edn., trs. J. D. Sinclair, OUP, 1961.

——, *The Divine Comedy*, trs. C. H. Sisson, Carcanet Press, 1980.

M. Deguy, 'A Draft of Several Reflections' (on *Shoah*), *Sulfur* 25, 1989.

S. Ezrahi, *By Words Alone*, Chicago U.P., 1980.

G. Hartman (ed.), *Bitburg in Moral and Political Perspective*, Indiana U.P. 1986.

E. Heimler, *Night of the Mist*, Vanguard Press, 1959.

——, *The Storm*, trs. A. Rudolph, The Menard Press, 1976.

E. Jabès, *A Share of Ink*, trs. A. Rudolf, The Menard Press, 1976.

V. Jankélévitch, *l'Imprescriptible*, Le Seuil, 1986.

L. Langer, *The Holocaust and the Literary Imagination*, Yale U.P. 1975.

C. Lanzmann, *Shoah*, Pantheon, 1985.

A. Momigliano, 'The Jews of Italy', *New York Review of Books*, October 24, 1985.

P. Rawicz, *Le Sang du ciel*, Gallimard, 1961.

——, *Blood from the Sky*, Secker and Warburg, 1964.

A. Rosenfeld, *A Double Dying*, Indiana U.P. 1980.

R. Rubinstein, *The Cunning of History*, Harper Colophon, 1978.

A. Rudolf, 'An I for a Thou', *New Humanist* 103/3, 1988.

——, 'Remembering the Future', *Jewish Quarterly* 37/1, 1990.

M. Ryle, *Martin Ryle's Letter*, ed. Michael Rowan-Robinson, The Menard Press, 1985.

A. Schwartz-Bart, *The Last of the Just*, Secker and Warburg, 1961.

J. Sobol, *Ghetto*, Nick Hern Books, 1989.

G. Steiner, *Language and Silence*, Faber and Faber, 1967.

R. Travers Herford, ed. and trs., *Sayings of the Fathers*, Schocken Books, NY, 1975.

J. Weil, *Life with a Star*, Collins, 1989.

E. Wiesel, *Night*, Hill and Wang, 1960.

M. Winick, ed. *Hunger Disease: Studies by the Jewish Physicians in the Warsaw Ghetto*, Wiley-Interscience, NY, 1979.

Y. H. Yerushalmi, *Zakhor: Jewish History and Jewish Memory*, Univ. Washington Press, 1982.